SPACED OUT

SPACE POEMS CHOSEN BY

BRIAN MOSES & JAMES CARTER

BLOOMSBURY EDUCATION

LONDON   OXFORD   NEW YORK   NEW DELHI   SYDNEY

For SG, the star-starter – JC

*For pupils and staff at Punnetts Town
CEP School, East Sussex, where I am their
Patron of Reading – BM*

CONTENTS

LOOKING UP

The Shooting Stars *James Carter* — 3

The Point *A.F. Harrold* — 4

Don't Just Google the Night Sky *Joan McLellan* — 5

Tonight *David Harmer* — 6

Grains of Sand *Dom Conlon* — 8

Moon Cat *Julie Douglas* — 9

The Winter Moon and the Willow *Clare Bevan* — 10

Total Eclipse *Valerie Bloom* — 12

Playing With Stars *Brian Moses* — 13

Walking to the Stars *Roger Stevens* — 15

Space Poem *James Carter* — 17

THE MOON AND THE SUN

Moon *A.F. Harrold* — 20

from The Moon Was But a Chin of Gold *Emily Dickinson* — 21

The Moon Speaks! *James Carter* — 22

Only the Moon *Wong May* — 23

Old Moon *Bernard Young* — 24

Silver Song *B.J. Lee* — 26

Tiny Moon *Zaro Weil* — 27

From One Moon *Dom Conlon* — 28

Moon Landing: July 20th 1969 *James Carter* — 29

First Dog on the Moon *David Orme* — 31

Moonscape *Judith Nicholls* — 32

George, Don't Do That *Bernard Young* — 33

The Sun and the Hare *Dom Conlon* 35

The Aged Sun *J. Patrick Lewis* 36

EIGHT PLANETS, A BILLION STARS

What Are the Great Eight? *James Carter* 38

Thank You, Planet Theia... *James Carter* 39

The Intergalactic Holiday Bus *Brian Moses* 41

The Rise and Fall of Pluto *Philip Waddell* 43

Planet So-So *Pauline Stewart* 45

Miranda the Frankenstein Moon *Coral Rumble* 47

Fishes Are Stars *Berlie Doherty* 48

Stars *Pie Corbett* 49

Headfirst Into Stars *Karen G. Jordan* 50

Stargrazing *John Rice* 51

Stars *Sue Hardy-Dawson* 52

BLACK HOLES AND OTHER DARK MATTERS

Black Hole *Liz Brownlee* 56

Black Hole *Jane Clarke* 57

Recipe for Cosmic Cupcakes *Julie Douglas* 58

Galactic Waltz *Tracey Mathias* 60

Perseids *Sue Dymoke* 61

Perseids *Carrie Finison* 62

Comet Song *Elli Woollard* 63

Dazzle Dance *Sue Hardy-Dawson* 64

Orange Star *Linda Lee Welch* 65

Space Junk *Joshua Seigal* 66

The Monster That Ate the Universe *Roger Stevens* 68

Bang? *Robert Schechter* 70

Universal Haiku Quartet *James Carter* 71

Last Chance *Kate Snow* 72

ALIEN LIFE

Imagine... *Penny Kent* 74

The Great Galactic Ghoul *Brian Moses* 75

Scalien *Paul Cookson* 77

Welcome *Trevor Millum* 79

Flight From Planet Earth *David Harmer* 80

Space Doubt *Graham Denton* 81

The Aliens *Brian Moses* 83

Old As New *James Carter* 85

SCIENCE AND SPACE TRAVEL

Now... *James Carter* 88

Discs and Dishes *John Mole* 89

The History of Nothing *David Harmer* 90

Galileo (1564–1642) *Chrissie Gittins* 92

The Big Bang *J. Patrick Lewis* 94

Space Dog *Brian Moses* 95

Earthling! Do You Know What You Are? *James Carter* 97

The First Man In Space *Graham Denton* 98

The International Space Station Above Our House *John Rice* 99

A Star Called Christa *Debra Bertulis* 101

The First Baby Born In Space *John Rice* 102

The First Cosmonaut *Dom Conlon* 104

Astronaut School *Brian Moses* 106

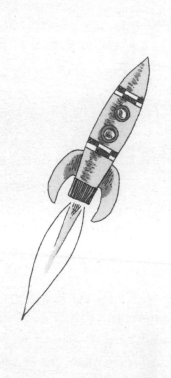

LOOKING UP

THE SHOOTING STARS

That night
we went out in the dark
and saw the shooting stars
was one of the best nights ever

It was as if someone
was throwing paint
across the universe

The stars just kept coming
and we 'oohed' and 'aahed'
like on bonfire night

And it didn't matter
they weren't real stars –
just bits of dust on fire
burning up in the atmosphere

And we stayed out there for ages
standing on this tiny planet
staring up at the vast cosmos

And I shivered
with the thrill
of it all

James Carter

THE POINT

Point to the sky.
Draw a line from your finger.
It'll go on forever.
Through light and through darkness.
Past astronauts sleeping.
Past clouds and past planets.
Through silence unmeasured.
Through time uncounted.
A line that's so long.
It will never stop going.
Long after you've dropped
Your hand to your side.
And gone back indoors.
That line is still sketching.
Onwards and outwards.
Universe threading.
Oh, your finger's a marvel.
Take care where you point it.

A.F. Harrold

DON'T JUST GOOGLE THE NIGHT SKY

Wrap up warm and go outside, out into the darkness,
Lie down and let the night air wrap around you.
Then look up, look all about, look up at the sky.
Let your eyes roam and sift through the patterns that emerge,
And take in the biggest dot-to-dot puzzle in the universe.
The solar system: the nearer planets, the outer planets.
The stars: double stars, variable stars, star clusters and nebulae.
The galaxy: comets and asteroids, meteors and moons,
Laid out as far as the eye can see and tantalisingly beyond,
All in the fullest glory of the human eye: no televisual fantasy,
No computer enhanced artist's impression composing possibilities.
View the moon's fullest phase as a blue or super, a harvest or blood;
A second orbital body where footprints mark the ground.
Follow the planetary calendar; their rising and waning
In a timeless dance around the sun, captive in its embrace.
What you see is what is real, up there in existence with us,
And it's existing with or without you looking,
With or without you caring,
with or without you.

So don't just google the night sky; go out, look up, be amazed!

Joan McLellan

TONIGHT

I'm looking out
of my bedroom window,
open-mouthed,
as thick cloud-clusters
turn from indigo,
to violet, then black.

The newly minted
moon stares down,
his cratered face pulls
a rocky grin,
as a scattered dust of stars,
suns, planets and galaxies
vibrates in front of me.

I see the red glow of Mars
the tiny emerald of Venus.
The Great Bear rumbles
above the darkened
line of trees.

Orion hunts, his mighty
silver sword gleaming,
Taurus the Bull stabs
long horns into the night,
his dancing eyes shimmer.

Every night this light show
is free, just look up there,
see for yourself, realise
just how small we are,
living on this blue globe
spinning round and round
the sun's burning eye.

David Harmer

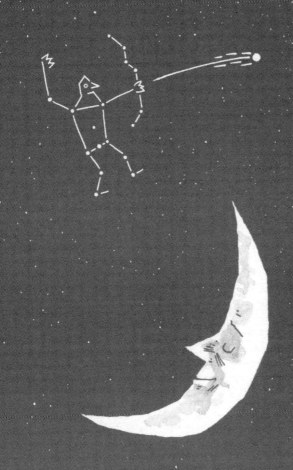

GRAINS OF SAND

There are more stars
in the universe
than there are grains
of sand on every beach
our seas have ever seen.

But only you
and only I
can feel that sand
between our toes
or see those stars
before our eyes.

Dom Conlon

MOON CAT

Moon Cat sits by the twisted tree
watching for twitchety tails.
Moon Cat purrs and cleans and preens.
Crescent moon on jet-black fur.
Moon Cat glistens.
Moon Cat listens.
Midnight paws poised to pounce.
Moon Cat melts into the shadows
and disappears with the sun.

Julie Douglas

THE WINTER MOON
AND THE WILLOW

Dear Moon,
I shook my tendrils to tangle you,
Trap you,
As you floated by.
I only wanted to keep you safe,
Let you rest in my branchy cage.

And for one enchanted moment
You balanced
On my tightrope of twigs,
Without fear or wonder.

But you were only playing your old tricks.

Soon you splashed my drooping arms
With your silver scribbles –
So bright, so cold.
I shivered, slipped my grip,
And set you free.

Now I watch you climb
The Pathway of Night,
Until you soar like a winter moth
On invisible wings,
Up and away.

Already, you have forgotten me.

Cruel Moon,
You have left me here,
Alone and lonely.
The grey mist
Drips.
I weep.
I weep.

Clare Bevan

January 2017
On one magical night, we saw two lunar wonders.
Our winter moon was both a Blue Moon and a Super Moon –
and for a moment, it was caught in the branches of a Weeping Willow.

TOTAL ECLIPSE

An eerie light haloes the treetops,
The nightingale ceases to sing,
The owl's eyes open, dilated,
Starlings tuck their heads under their wings.

A cold wind awakes from the waters,
Walks mournfully over the sand,
And the darkness, swift as a flash flood,
Covers the face of the land.

The earth holds its breath in wonder,
The silence complete, unbroken,
And there's a tiny glimpse of the way it was
Before the world was spoken.

Valerie Bloom

PLAYING WITH STARS

Young children know what it's like
to play with stars.

First of all it's a wink and a smile
from some distant constellation,
then it's hide-and-seek as they disappear
in a cover of cloud.
Sometimes children see how far
they can travel to a star
before familiar voices call them
home to bed.

Like all good games, of course,
you need to use a little imagination
when playing with stars.
More experienced players
can jump over stars
or shake down a star.
Some can trap them in butterfly nets,
but you should always let them loose again –
stars grow pale and die if you cage them.

Sometimes the stars tell stories
of their journeys across the sky,
and sometimes they stay silent.
At these times children may travel themselves,
wandering a line that unravels
through their dreams.
At these times too, the stars play their own games,
falling from the sky when there's no one there
to catch them.

Sometimes you find these stars on the ground,
dazed, confused. Be warned though,
even fallen stars may be hot to touch.

Young children know what it's like
to rescue stars, to hold them gently
in gloved hands and then,
with one almighty fling,
sling them back to the sky.

Adults forget what it's like
to play with stars,
and when children offer to teach them,
they're far too busy.

Brian Moses

WALKING TO THE STARS

Sometimes it feels
like you can touch the moon,
reach out with your finger
and touch it,
when the sky is bright
on a clear cold night.

Likewise the stars.
They seem so close
you could almost breathe them in.

And sometimes you feel
as if you could walk to the moon
across an invisible starlit bridge.
And I know that we can't walk to the moon,
but if we could...
How long would it take?

Well, walking non-stop, about
eighty thousand hours.
That's nine years.

And what if, when you reached the moon,
you thought you might continue your journey
and walk across the galaxy to the nearest star?
How long would that take?

In years? More than nine. Here's the figure.
Take a deep breath now.
8,000,000,000,000 years.
That's a very long walk.

Some journeys, I think,
are too far
to even contemplate.

Roger Stevens

SPACE POEM

The **sun** is like
a gold balloon

    the **moon**
    a silver pearl

the **earth** is like
a marble blue

    the **milky way**
    a creamy swirl.

If **stars** are like
those little boats

    afloat a sea
    of **night**

the **dark** is when
a hand comes down

    and switches
    off the **light**...

James Carter

THE MOON
AND THE SUN

MOON

Coming out of school
and there she is
a chalk smudge
finger dab
of white on blue.
You can see the sky through it
like
your mother's heart
through her frown.

A.F. Harrold

from THE MOON WAS BUT A CHIN OF GOLD

The moon was but a Chin of Gold
A Night or two ago –
And now she turns Her perfect Face
Upon the World below –

Emily Dickinson

THE MOON SPEAKS!

I, the moon,
would *like it known – I*
never *follow people home. I*
simply do *not have the time. And*
neither do *I ever shine. For what you*
often see at *night is me reflecting solar*
light. And *I'm not cheese! No, none of*
these: no mozz*arellas, cheddars, bries, all*
you'll find *here – if you please – are my*
dusty, empty *seas. And cows do not*
jump over *me. Now that is simply*
lunacy! *You used to come and*
visit me. *Oh do return,*
I'm lonely, *see.*

James Carter

ONLY THE MOON

When I was a child I thought
the new moon was a cradle
The full moon was granny's round face.

The new moon was a banana
The full moon was a big cake.

When I was a child
I never saw the moon
I only saw what I wanted to see.

And now I see the moon
It's the moon
Only the moon, and nothing but the moon.

Wong May

OLD MOON

Moon is older than history.

It was there at the beginning.

It's much much much much older than you, child.

And yes, it's even older
than white-haired old me!

It's ancient.
It's wondrous.

More ancient
than the Ancient Egyptians.

More wondrous than the pyramids.

Tutankhamun will have looked up at it.
So will all of those folk working hard to build the pyramids.

And Florence Nightingale.
And Marie Curie.

And Julius Caesar.
And Gandhi.

And Stone Age man.
And woman.

And howling wolves and dinosaurs.

And mums and dads and grannies and grandads,
and all of their mums and dads and grannies and grandads,
and all of theirs and theirs and theirs and theirs
and so on.

Your teachers will have examined it.
Your friends will all have stared at it.

Shakespeare and J.K. Rowling and Roald Dahl and Walt Disney
and anyone else you care to mention
will have seen it.

All over the world everyone knows about the moon,
the wondrous moon,
the marvellous moon.

Everyone knows about it,
and keeps an eye on it.

Bernard Young

SILVER SONG

Moon, peer in my window
and sing a silver song.
Your lullaby of gentle light
will linger all night long.

Moon, shine in my window
and sing in your voice deep
a midnight song of moonbeams
to rock me safe to sleep.

B.J. Lee

TINY MOON

Tiny moon

Even a
Penny
Could eclipse you
This morning

Zaro Weil

FROM ONE MOON

they look across
at the distant earth
tiny and marbled
like a glassblower's egg
and wonder
how seven billion people
could emerge
from that

I look back
squint-eyed through the ring
of my finger and thumb
and think of how
two astronauts
pecking in the dust
can make
a whole world
look up

Dom Conlon

MOON LANDING: JULY 20TH 1969

for Betty

To celebrate
the first moonwalk
I invented
my own TV

All it took
was a cardboard box
two bottle tops
a spot of glue
and some paper –
on which I drew
an astronaut
on top of a bright
blue moon

The whole family
came to our house
for the day

And for a moment
the world
stopped turning
we all
stopped breathing
as we watched
those fuzzy pictures
and heard
those crackly voices
travelling thousands
of miles through space
as those two men
stepped down

and took those leaps
    in the lunar
        sand

My aunty
said my TV
was better
than the real thing –
so she moved it
into the window
so everyone
could see
my paper moon

James Carter

FIRST DOG ON THE MOON

'Hi there,
First Dog on the Moon,
How do you feel?'

Like nothing on Earth.

'Yes, but can you taste anything up there?'

*Bones so cold and dry
They bite my tongue.*

'That's great, First Dog on the Moon.
Now what can you smell?'

*Fear of the things hiding in
Hard shadows.*

'OK, OK, so what can you see?'

*Long dead forests,
Broken winds in empty streets,
Things,
Shadows.*

'So what are you going to do next,
First Dog on the Moon?'

Sit and howl at the earth.

David Orme

MOONSCAPE

No air, no mist, no man, no beast.

No water flows from her Sea of Showers,

no trees, no flowers fringe her Lake of Dreams.

No grass grows or clouds shroud her high hills

or deep deserts. No whale blows in her dry

Ocean of Storms.

Judith Nicholls

GEORGE, DON'T DO THAT

In an old black and white movie
called *It's a Wonderful Life*
a character named George Bailey
says to Mary, his future wife,

'You want the moon? Just say the word
and I'll throw a lasso round it
and bring it down.'

But if George did that
the moon's gravitational pull
would cause a huge tidal bulge
which would be dreadful;

low tides would get lower,
high tides would get higher,
and as the moon got even nearer,
close enough for us to wave at and shout *Hiya!*,

it would exert a gravitational force
400 times greater than we're used to.
There would be large-scale flooding.
Cities such as London and New

York would disappear under water.
There would be earthquakes. Volcanoes
would erupt. Our wonderful lives
would be pretty messed up. Those

are not good things to think about (though they would suit a disaster movie. Very dramatic!). Clearly, George was not considering such matters when he was getting all romantic!

Bernard Young

THE SUN AND THE HARE

When Sun was young
he rode the earth on Hare's back.
Hot as thoughtlessness
he burned and Hare bucked and leaped,
crossing mountains and myths,
ice ages and oceans until,
jealous of a volcano, Sun eased
into the foothills, dismounted, and
was about to drink the land dry
when he noticed Hare's brown fur
glowing golden. Angry, but unable
to become incandescent, he tried
to reclaim what he thought was his.
But Hare was too fast,
slipping away like Sun's youth.

Dom Conlon

THE AGED SUN

Whether our star, the sun, grows old
by turning into liquid gold

And dripping down invisible space
to some celestial fireplace,

Expands, like science says it must,
and turns its planets into dust,

Or simply ups and disappears
like some ascending-ending spheres,

I do not think it matters much.
Great things destroy, depart, lose touch

When slow time reckons they are done –
and so it will be with the sun.

J. Patrick Lewis

EIGHT PLANETS,
A BILLION STARS

WHAT ARE THE GREAT EIGHT?

There's MERCURY, VENUS
there's EARTH and MARS
the first four planets
around our star

There's JUPITER, SATURN
URANUS too
then NEPTUNE's next
and last, mind you...

Now read this rhyme
and over again,
you'll soon know all
THE EIGHT by name!

James Carter

THANK YOU, PLANET THEIA...

... for hurtling through
the universe,
for slamming
into early Earth,
for smashing rocks
that formed
the fiery moon –
    that year by year
        would nudge away
        and cool
           to dusty grey.

But you're a theory,
not a fact,
your story's called
The Big Whack –
that tells one way
you may have made
our moon.

We need that moon
for tides, for light,
for company
on winter nights.

So, Theia –
    if your tale is true –
                  we
                     must
                        thank
                         you!

James Carter

THE INTERGALACTIC HOLIDAY BUS

The Intergalactic Holiday Bus
got lost on the byways of Mars.
The driver was out of practice
at navigating by stars.
His satnav broke and the bus took off
in completely the wrong direction
and when 'turn around' became possible,
they were late for their next connection.

They'd miss the storm clouds of Jupiter
if they waited for the next ship
that would take them on to Saturn
where they could rejoin their trip.
And they'd miss the special excursion
to one of Jupiter's moons
where some overactive volcano
was sending out sulphur plumes.

Still, they'd be in time to go skating
round one of Saturn's rings
then on to gas giant Uranus
with the colder weather it brings.
Warm clothes would then be needed
for planet Neptune too,
but they wouldn't be visiting Pluto,
there are far better things to do.

So, all in all, it wasn't too bad,
leaving the tourist track,
and the sights they'd missed this time
would later tempt them back.
But on the postcards they wrote
to their relatives back home,
all were in total agreement –
next year it's Paris or Rome.

Brian Moses

THE RISE AND FALL OF PLUTO

I'd been hanging around
the Kuiper neighbourhood unnoticed
until Earth year 1930 when,
out of the blue, I was spotted
along with my potential
and immediately recruited.

Okay I would only be number 9
but at last I was recognised,
respected,
one of the gang,
one of the big guys,
one of the planets.

And I've never changed,
hardly aged,
I'm still as fit,
but then they notice a few other bods
in my neighbourhood
they reckon to be almost as worthy
and get particularly impressed with this Eris,
and just because Eris is a bit bigger
they decide to demote me, dismiss me, diss me.

Well makes no difference,
I'm still around,
I ain't going nowhere.

Call me a minor planet if you like,
I don't care,
I ain't bothered,
sticks and stones...

Philip Waddell

Pluto was discovered in 1930 by the American astronomer Clyde Tombaugh

PLANET SO-SO

Imagine a planet
   far out in space
               where
one kind of people
                    live
in one kind of
            place.
One kind of
              language,
one kind of flower,
   days which last for
only one hour.
   This planet has
                  one
so-so star.
The people there
play
one-string
              guitars.

The so-so people tell
one
        so-so joke
about a cold cup
                                    of
tea
            and
                        an artichoke.
The weather
                        forecast
        is always bleak,
        beneath their
so-so cloud called
                    Unique.

Pauline Stewart

MIRANDA THE FRANKENSTEIN MOON

There's nothing as strange, showing unexplained change,
Than Miranda the Frankenstein moon,
In the shade of Uranus, she's not very famous,
Though she glows like a silver-pink spoon.

With her broken terrain and tempestuous name,
She's a haphazard patchwork, much scarred.
She's disfigured, unsightly (I can't put it politely),
But a mystery we can't disregard.

With her craters and grooves and tectonic moves,
With her canyons and unexplored belly,
She's an icy-cold riddle, with rock in the middle –
But she would have inspired Mary Shelley.

Coral Rumble

FISHES ARE STARS

Fishes are stars
they swarm in constellations
angels, trailing long fins

The ghost fish is a moon
flying fish leap like shooting stars
babies nest in their Milky Way of bubbles
neons gleam blue, red, green

Like the winking lights of planets, years away.

Berlie Doherty

STARS

are to reach for,
beautiful freckles of hope,
speckles on velvet,
to steer ships,
to comfort those trapped in the darkness of their making,
to lead the wayward when the compass falters,
to remind us that the day is almost breaking,
dawn is just out – taking time to warm the other side of the
    earth.

Stars are for wishes.

Stars are
tiny lights of hope,
fireflies in the night,
golden specks to gaze at,
tin tacks on a dark cloth,
studs glittering,
sequins on a first party dress.

Stars are
our brightest and best,
shards of hope to keep us going,
marking the place,
marking the seasons, giving us purpose,
because somewhere out there

there are other stargazers
gazing back.

Pie Corbett

HEADFIRST INTO STARS

Upon a lake,
upon a dock,
upon a moonless night,
I raised my eyes: a star-streaked sky
held endless sparks of light.

It made me gasp,
it made me sway,
it made me look below.
I saw a million stars there too,
a mesmerising show.

I took a breath,
I took a leap,
I took a headfirst dive.
I splashed around in stars that night,
and laughed to be alive.

Karen G. Jordan

STARGRAZING

If the sun was made of birthday cake
   I'd eat at least six slices.
If the moon was made of marmalade
   ah, sweet oranges and spices.

If space was made of lemonade
   to swim would be amazing.
If stars were tiny lollipops
   I'd spend my nights stargrazing!

John Rice

STARS

A boy once thought
that stars were glass
afraid they'd shatter
if anyone passed
he dreamt that clouds
were made of rag.

A girl once thought
stars were diamonds
worried the dark had
come to steal them
she dreamt a crown
to set their stones in.

A boy once thought
that stars were paper
anxious they'd scatter
on the windblown air
he dreamt he caught
them in nets of silver.

A girl once thought
stars scars in heaven
she lay awake often
dreading their healing
she dreamt of scissors
that keep the sky open.

A boy once thought
that stars were ice
fearing cold rain
on summer nights
he dreamt a moon frost
to keep hard their light.

A girl knew for certain
that stars were just gas
and she slept very warm
in her fearless bed
but she dreamt of nothing
so I mention her last.

Sue Hardy-Dawson

BLACK HOLES
AND OTHER
DARK MATTERS

BLACK HOLE

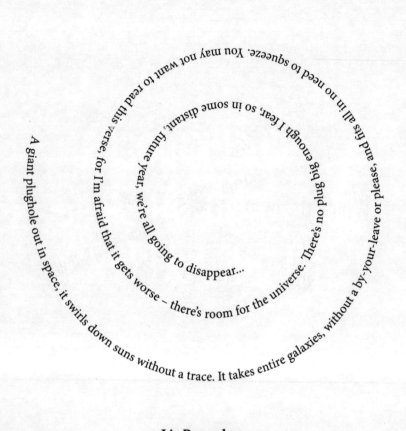

A giant plughole out in space, it swirls down suns without a trace. It takes entire galaxies, without a by-your-leave or please, without a by-your-leave or please. There's no plug big enough I fear, so in some distant, future year, we're all going to disappear... for I'm afraid that it gets worse – there's room for the universe. You may not want to read this verse, for I'm afraid that it gets worse – there's room for the universe.

Liz Brownlee

BLACK HOLE

Jane Clarke

RECIPE FOR COSMIC CUPCAKES

Crumble a cluster of comets and a shower of meteorites
Over a supernova, glittering and bright.

Sprinkle on some Pluto particles, using a galactic grater.
Mix together with a solar spoon in the deepest Martian crater.

Into your celestial concoction, pop a star from Orion's Belt.
Choose a layer of ozone. Use a sunbeam to gently melt.

Carefully gather a pinch of gravity and some atmosphere – just
    a dash.
Under the light of a constellation, select a moon to mash.

Pick the darkest, blackest hole. Chop and finely slice.
Catch a passing asteroid. Peel, quarter and roughly dice.

Add a luminous nebula. Stir in a scoop of Milky Way.
Keep whisking at the speed of light. Bake with a cosmic ray.

Each cupcake needs a topping of moon dust. Now they are
    ready to eat.
Serve on a flying saucer and enjoy the universe's sweetest treat.

Julie Douglas

GALACTIC WALTZ

Galaxies sing while Andromeda dances,
And Hercules waltzes with Cassiopeia.
Give me your hand,
and we'll spin
To the silvery music that rings
From celestial spheres.

Birds of the night shower feathers of star-shine,
A glimmering, shimmering falling of light.
Give me your hand,
and we'll fly
With Columba, Aquila and Cygnus
Far into the night.

Infinite fire in the darkness above us
Where Draco and Phoenix flame, flicker and burn.
Give me your hand:
we will dance
With the stars to the end of the night,
And we'll never return.

Tracey Mathias

*This poem was originally written as one of a suite of songs,
for the Da Capo Music Foundation summer school in 2012*

PERSEIDS

Flare in thin air

Flit high above moonlit earth

Sudden shafts of light

Faster than rockets

Take us by surprise

Better than fireworks

Dodging stars

Burst in a blaze

Zip... zip... zip open the dark

Shoot out from the deep

Turn space into a moving dot-to-dot

Dazzle planets

Their flaming tails smudge out darkness

Keep us guessing

A million Bolts sprint a sparkling
100 metres

Beam their lightsabre blades across lonely places

Mesmerising meteors

Flashes of white-hot fire

Keep us spellbound

Magic wands illuminating August nights

Before their light takes flight

And they are gone...

Sue Dymoke

PERSEIDS

One August night
as black as anything
and nothing,
we lay in grass damp with dew
and watched you,
miles high,
streak across the sky.
Your fate: not to constellate
but to drop

down,

down,

to disintegrate
into dust,

and disappear.

(Until next year.)

Carrie Finison

The annual Perseid meteor shower is caused by debris from the Swift-Tuttle comet, which burns up as it travels through Earth's atmosphere. It is usually at its peak in August. Find a very dark spot away from city lights, lie back and watch the show!

COMET SONG

What does a comet sing of?
What's in the hum and the thrum of its sound
As it blazes its way through the black all around?
Does it sing of the empty and infinite night,
Of the vast lonely void stretching far out of sight?
Does it sing of the fury of fire? Does it cry
Of the awe and the wonder of star-studded sky?
Does it roar at the terrible beauty? Or chime
With the long-distant music of time before time?
Does it sing of new worlds as they sizzle and spark?
Or only of nothing, a fathomless dark?
And then, as it speeds on its journey through space,
Does it sing of the tickle from Earth on its face?

Elli Woollard

DAZZLE DANCE

I am made of heat and light
comets spinning through the night
spit and splinter – meteorite
firecracker, pinwheel bright.

I am made from ash and coal
watch my embers wax and glow
twist and turn my body so
dragon breath to volcano.

I have frazzle crackle hands
dance a razzle dazzle dance
simmer swirling twist and prance
glitter, sparkle to entrance.

I am made of cinder stars
gases burning from afar
supernova in the dark
flash of thunder full of spark.

I incinerate and blaze
candles burning in my gaze
born of fire, heat and flame
come and bask beneath my rays.

Sue Hardy-Dawson

ORANGE STAR

February 14, 3001
Aldebaran/Alpha Tauri

Greetings Mother!
And Happy Love Day.
I'm sitting in the solopod
imagining the party back at home
on Earth Two (shame about the first one).
It's hot here in the heart of Taurus
but the AC works most days.
I'm lonely, but have got very good
at talking to myself
and the Pleiades through the window
though it's seldom we agree
on much of anything.
Have fun, dear Mum, and
– sometimes –
                    think of me.

XXX Your Maia

Linda Lee Welch

SPACE JUNK

They say
that bits of rusty satellite
float around
the sky at night,

that up there, just beyond
the earth's atmosphere,
hunks of broken debris
drift forlornly.

So I look up and think:
what else
might be stuck there
longing for warmth and love?

An alien's
homesick teddy, perhaps,
or an astronaut cut loose
from her spaceship.

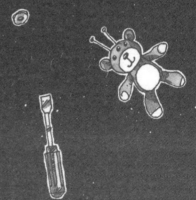

Maybe there's a block
of cosmic moon-cheese,
or the spent match
that lit the Big Bang.

If I squint hard enough
I think I can make out
Saturn's missing
wedding ring

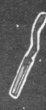

and a lost
love letter
from Neptune
to Pluto

just beyond
the earth's atmosphere
up there
              drifting.

Joshua Seigal

THE MONSTER THAT ATE THE UNIVERSE

I began with a pancake.
But why stop there?
So I ate the spoon
And the table and chair.

What's my name?
The Monster That Ate the Universe

I ate all the cutlery.
I ate the cheese grater.
The cooker. The microwave.
The refrigerator.

What's my name?
The Monster That Ate the Universe.

I wolfed down the kitchen.
The dining room too.
I slurped up the bathroom
Including the loo.

What's my name?
The Monster That Ate the Universe.

I chewed up the house.
I gulped it all down.
I ate the whole street.
Then I swallowed the town.

What's my name?
The Monster That Ate the Universe.

I devoured the country.
Then what do you think?
I drank all the ocean.
I needed a drink.

What's my name?
The Monster That Ate the Universe.

Then the earth I consumed,
The planets, the sun.
I was still feeling peckish
And having such fun.

What's my name?
The Monster That Ate the Universe.

So I gorged on the galaxy.
Then the galaxy next door.
I was still feeling hungry
So I gobbled up more.

What's my name?
The Monster That Ate the Universe.

I dined on them all
As the prophets all feared.
Then I swallowed myself
And (burp!) disappeared.

In the silence that followed
A little bird sang.
Then nothing. Just silence.
And a very big **BANG!**

Roger Stevens

BANG?

When the Big Bang banged
there was nobody near it.
No one existed
so no one could hear it,

and there was no air
to be anywhere found,
nothing to vibrate
or carry the sound.

So how can they say
when the universe sprang
from nothing to something
it made a big bang?

Robert Schechter

UNIVERSAL HAIKU QUARTET

LUNAR

Glare of cold silver
belly of ancient stardust
face of an old ghost!

STELLAR

Hey, look up humans,
high in the temple of night –
such cosmic candles!

SOLAR

So what don't you make
in your fiery factory?
Light, heat, even... *life!*

EARTHLY

A precious blue stone
a slowly spinning sapphire
the rock we call *home...*

James Carter

LAST CHANCE

Sunshine	Melts away, frightened, when the cursing	cometS
Take	Over the dark blue	nighT
Asteroids argue	Over who's the strongest	A
Red giant star boasts of its	Night brightness with a mighty	roaR
Light years below, a	Broken-hearted earth lies	stilL
It whispers, 'I'm	Expiring, hurting, burning but	I
Guess no one's listening	Any more: I'm slowly	dyinG
Help me, please:	Make me a promise as I	diminisH
Tell me the	Stars will never go	ouT'

Kate Snow

ALIEN LIFE

IMAGINE...

My first could be hostile, it's always in space.
My second's in films, with an unearthly face.
My third is in weird and also in sonic.
My fourth is in freakish; it's sometimes bionic.
My fifth's in antennae and tentacles – look!
My whole might be purple or green in a book.

Penny Kent

THE GREAT GALACTIC GHOUL

*A fictional space monster that was reputed
to survive on a diet of Mars space probes*

Don't fool around with the great galactic ghoul,
it's not the sort of creature to play by the rules.
For any spaceship sent its way
will not return to Earth some day.
It will simply bat it out of the sky,
splat it hard just like a fly.

This ghoul was never taught right from wrong,
it lives by its muscles, is incredibly strong.
It's ugly as Medusa whose snakes have just woken,
with a nose like a boxer's that's regularly broken.
Eyes like saucers, the flying kind,
acts like a creature that's lost its mind.

And the great galactic ghoul
does very little but slobber and drool
as it shuffles about on the edge of Mars
and anyone flying in from the stars
should beware the ghoul, stay clear of its lair
or it might just swing you round by your hair,
then squeeze you between its loathsome jaws
till it swallows you, rubs its belly and ROARS.

P.S. It lives a long way from you
and that's where it usually stays.
But something's wrong, the ghoul has gone,
and it hasn't been seen for days.

Brian Moses

SCALIEN

Scalien snakes through cosmic skies
Scalien scares and terrifies
Scalien scans through Scalien eyes
Ssssssscalien... Ssssssscalien

Scalien slaloms stars at night
Scalien squeezes spaceships tight
Scalien speeding fast as light
Ssssssscalien... Ssssssscalien

Scalien slips through space and time
Scalien scales – serpentine
Scalien shines on alien slime
Ssssssscalien... Ssssssscalien

Paul Cookson

WELCOME

I came to the Entry Desk.
She didn't look up.
She was behind a screen.

Name? she barked.
Arfgam Banghwam, I said.
Planet of Origin?
Varglewark 3.
Colour?
Pinky-brown.
Not green?
Not green.
She didn't look up.

Appendages?
I'm sorry?
Legs, tentacles, tails, etcetera.
Oh. Two arms, two legs.
She sighed.
Special antennae?
None.
Optical sensors?
Two eyes, brown.
Finally she looked up.

I'm sorry, you don't seem
Like an extra-terrestrial to me.
She looked disapproving, disbelieving.

I didn't want to disappoint her.
So I zapped her
With my third-brain sonic ray.
Bam!

She evaporated.
Satisfied? I asked.

Trevor Millum

FLIGHT FROM PLANET EARTH

Landing here because we had to
The fuel gone and the computers broken
We crashed into a bank of sand
Let the dust die down
Then climbed out of our rocket.

We were surrounded by eyes
Along the rim of the distant mountains
In the desert at our feet
It was worse at night
When they glowed like fires
Without blinking.

Time has passed
We live in the wreck of our spacecraft
Eat what is left of our stores
Drink rainwater
Sometimes we go out looking for food
The creatures always force us back
Make us afraid
We are the aliens here
And they don't like us.

David Harmer

SPACE DOUBT

When I asked Dad
if he believed
in UFOs, or flying saucers,
or alien spacecraft
of any sort,
he just laughed.
'Don't be daft,'
was his retort.

And when I asked him
if he thought
there might be life on other planets
like Pluto or Neptune or Jupiter,
my dad just shrugged his shoulders,
shook his head, and said,
'Pluto or Neptune or Jupiter?
I think you're getting stupider!'

And when I said to my dad,
'Dad, do you think we'll ever get visited
by strange beings
travelling in a rocket ship?' He
said, 'Now that's just plain silly.
You must think I'm a bit dippy!'

'To believe there's creatures from another race
somewhere deep in outer space,
I'd have to be completely mad,'
said Dad.

'Everyone knows,' he said,
'the only living beings
in all of the stars
are right here
on Mars.'

Graham Denton

THE ALIENS

They came to look round,
these alien visitors.

There were witnesses,
quite a few.

Some clearly unreliable,
partygoers, others
quite sober, taking
photographs, recording data.

There were differences
of opinion: Some saw circles
of light, some saw cigar-shaped
luminescence. Some talked of
shifts in position, some saw
smoke, flames. Everything
was noted down.

Some claimed the craft stayed still
while beams of light
criss-crossed the ground.
Some saw zigzagging,
spinning.

Some reckoned seconds,
others minutes, some say
they signalled a code, lighting
the road where cars were
stationary.

Onboard the craft it took
no time at all for the planet's
suitability to be dismissed.

After all, who would want to
settle somewhere
so polluted, so
inhospitable and
with such a short amount
of time before it became
uninhabitable.

Best continue searching,
but first deliver
a parting shot,
put the planet
out of its misery.

That would be best.

No worth at all to be found
in this place called
Earth.

Brian Moses

OLD AS NEW

How *old* are you?

W R O N G !

Everything young
  and everything new
    is really recycled *old*.

The **moon**
  was made
    from recycled
      earth.

The **earth**
  was made
    from recycled
      sun.

And *you?*

Your atoms
  were made
    when the **sun**
      was born.

And you thought
you were *young...?*

HEY, OLDIE –
        HAPPY
            4.76 BILLIONTH
                    BIRTHDAY!

James Carter

SCIENCE AND
SPACE TRAVEL

NOW...

The birth of a star.
The beat of a heart.

The arc of an hour.
The bee and the flower.

The flight of a swan.
The weight of the sun.

A river in flood.
The nature of blood.

The future in space
for this human race.

Now that's
what I call
s c i e n c e.

James Carter

DISCS AND DISHES

Hearing what I want to hear
I'm happy that the tuning's right
But when reception isn't clear
I blame it on the satellite.

The sky is full of discs and dishes
Thanks to Scientific Man –
Though outer space controls my wishes
Inner space is where I am.

John Mole

THE HISTORY OF NOTHING

'Once there was nothing,
then a pebble of gas and dust,
rock and atoms plus swirling,
fantastic energies all exploded
in a Big Bang!' said our teacher.

'My brain hurts,' whispered Sanjay.

'It made the universe,
which stretched and expanded,
growing bigger and bigger, creating
stars and suns, moons and planets,
like our planet Earth,' said our teacher.

'And dinosaurs?' asked Sanjay.

'Yes and humans later on
and oxygen, carbon dioxide, oceans,
clouds, skies and it didn't stop. It's still spinning
outwards, making black holes, new nebulae
and galaxies,' said our teacher.

'And aliens?' laughed Sanjay.

'Don't know about that,
Sanjay, but thank you for asking.
And there was nothing at all there before
this explosion, just empty darkness
going on forever,' said our teacher.

'What's nothing?' asked Sanjay

'Ten minus ten,' smiled Clever Chloe.
'But there must have been something
you can't just have nothing. Nothing is a Something
if that's all there is,' said Sanjay.
'Well there was nothing,' said our teacher.

'Now is that the bell?'

'I think they make this stuff up
to confuse us, even if it's true,' I said
on the yard but Sanjay wasn't listening,
he was playing football with Smigsy
so I went in goal

and we won five-nothing.

David Harmer

GALILEO (1564-1642)

I heard about the first telescope
being made in Holland – too far
away for me to see from Pisa,
but still, I made my own.
It was better.

I saw the mountains and valleys
of the moon, sunspots,
the four largest moons of Jupiter.

You might think you are the centre
of the universe,
and most people did,
but we revolve around the sun.

New ideas are hard to break.
I stuck to mine and was imprisoned.
First in jail, then in a villa
I could not leave.

Thought is slow to change.
I hold no grudge.
The truth will out

and in time I was named a father –
The Father of Modern Science.
Now my thoughts trip lightly
through the centuries.

Chrissie Gittins

THE BIG BANG

Well, we thank you, Edwin Hubble,
That you took the time and trouble
To investigate just how the world began –

Like a universal splatter,
An exploding poo-poo platter,
Or a zillion popcorn kernels in a pan.

How and why and when and whether
All the matter came together
Is a riddle not completely understood.

But there is a growing chorus –
Fifteen billion years before us,
Something definitely wrecked the neighbourhood!

J. Patrick Lewis

SPACE DOG

She must have been someone's pet,
sometime before the scientists
found her, tagged and labelled her
suitable for space.
She had, someone said,
a trusting face.

She must have been shocked
when the ones she'd trusted
strapped her down
in some strange contraption,
stroked her head, tickled
under her chin, then left,
and locked her in.

She must have been cowed
by the rocket's power,
shaken by the roar, the thrust
must have left her
shivering, with no one there
to calm her down
when she needed it most.

She must have whined
for a long time, while wires
taped to her skin
relayed her reactions.

She must have thought
it was some sort of game
gone painfully wrong
and that very soon they'd
release her.

She must have closed her eyes
when the temperature rose.
I hope she was thinking of trees,
of running through fields.

And if only they'd had the means
to bring her back,
she would have given them
her usual welcome,
forgiven them too,
like dogs forgive all humans,
the hurtful things we do.

Brian Moses

EARTHLING! DO YOU KNOW WHAT YOU ARE?

A
mammal
with a massive
brain. A mega
mass of **DNA.**
A **biped**
and
a
hominid*.*
!!   A **primate** *and a   !!*
!! **vertebrate***. A* **warm-** *!!*
!! **blooded omnivore** *with   !!*
!! **carbon molecules** *galore. And   !!*
!!   oh yeah, did you know – you are   !!
!!   mostly H2O? A star-deriving, time-   !!
!!   surviving, earth-evolving, space-   !!
!!   exploring, future-seeking,   !!
!!   ever-thinking, speaking,   !!
!!!!   breeding, breathing   !!!!
H U M A N
B E I N G ?
!!   !!
!!   !!
!!   !!
!!   !!
!!   !!
!!   !!
!!   !!
!!!!!!!   !!!!!!!

James Carter

THE FIRST MAN IN SPACE

Circling the earth
in an orbital spaceship,
he marvelled at the beauty
of our planet, saw
for the first time
its shape,
the folds of the terrain,
the shores of continents,
islands and great rivers
as well as large bodies of water.
It was, he declared
on his return,
a beauty
for the people of the world
to safeguard and enhance,
not destroy.
For the feelings which had filled him
as he flew
just a few miles up into the sky,
he could express with but one word –
joy.

Graham Denton

*On April 12 1961, 27-year-old Russian Cosmonaut, Flight Major Yuri
Gagarin became the first human to journey into outer space when his*
Vostok 1 *spacecraft completed an orbit of the earth. His flight lasted
108 minutes at a speed of 17,025 mph.*

THE INTERNATIONAL SPACE STATION ABOVE OUR HOUSE

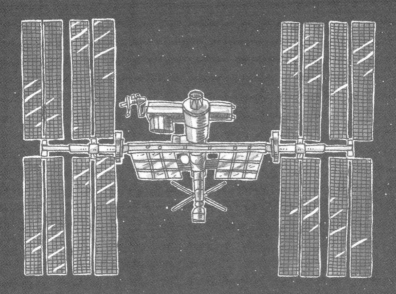

Daylight has toppled over the hills behind our house
and someone is painting the night a deep, dark blue.

My family and our neighbours gather in our garden –
the children are excited, the adults are a little bemused.

Everyone has questions; how high is it, what size is it, who's in it?
I wish I could answer but I know few facts – just the beauty of it.

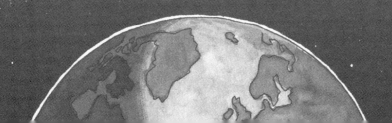

A speck of shy light high in the west; the enchantment begins
as the International Space Station glides gracefully into view.

The children scream with delight; even the adults are smiling
as out of the lonely wings of the west and into centre stage

this bewitching machine tiptoes silently, wondrously above us,
pointing to our future – our artificial angel.

John Rice

A STAR CALLED CHRISTA

There is an asteroid named Christa
And a crater on the moon
In memory of a teacher
Who lost her life too soon.

Christa was so excited
To have won the coveted place
The first U.S. civilian
To venture into space.

Millions of children watched in schools
Millions of children cried
As seventy-three seconds after launch
The dream that was hers had died.

There must be a star called Christa
A star that will never die
Beaming a ray of love and hope
To dreamers like you and I.

Debra Bertulis

In memory of Christa McAuliffe who died in the Space Shuttle
Challenger disaster on January 28th 1986

THE FIRST BABY BORN IN SPACE

The Shuttle brought a midwife.
Her first time in space, she had fainted at takeoff;
not because she was afraid or poorly trained,
but because she was overwhelmed by the event.

A flight into space is like a journey into
your own true being – it can be frighteningly beautiful.

By the time they docked and boarded Rockfield 12,
everyone aboard the station was anxious and edgy.
The Captain was in labour, she had been for four hours,
and everyone could sense Space Baby was due soon;
(Space Baby was not just the crew's nickname for him/her,
every newspaper on Earth was using that name!)

Special equipment was unloaded from the Shuttle
and the midwife set about her practised work
within a specially constructed, huge plastic bubble.

Outside stars drifted by as gently
as would distant house lights viewed from a train.
Normal life on board the space station was suspended
as Space Baby's arrival edged closer.
It was a nervous time for everyone;
The men of the crew rubbed the stubble on their chin,
the women of the crew drummed their fingers
on their keyboards leaving a meaningless trail of
lkjhlkjhlkjhlkjhlkjklkjhlkjhlkjhlkjhlkjhlkjhlkjhlkjhlkjhlkjhlkj
confusing the computer.
Everyone had a coffee within reach –
minutes passed as slowly as those stars outside.

And then it happened, the familiar bing-bong-bing
from the ship's loudspeakers followed by an unsteady,
nervous announcement from the communications section:
'Spacemen, spacewomen, astronauts, cosmonauts, taikonauts.
We are pleased to announce that Rockfield 12
is the birthplace of the world's first Space Child,
a little girl, Najima, born two minutes ago.
Mother (indeed Captain) and daughter doing well.
Our congratulations to Najima's father who has been
watching the birth of his daughter via direct video link
to his home in Kenya.

Ladies and gentlemen, travelling down the birth canal
was one short trip for a newborn child,
a giant journey for humankind. Welcome to history!'

John Rice

THE FIRST COSMONAUT

Travel through life
as though life is the cosmos

as though you are the first person
to fly into its void

as though your outstretched arms
are powered by the sun

as though your body
is the mathematics of freedom

as though your fingers
speak the only language there is

as though your eyes
are newborn stars in a nebula

as though your heart
can survive a supernova

as though each day
is a new planet

as though each year
is weightless

as though each moment
is an atom

as though solitude
is fuel

as though even if you land
you will always fly again

Dom Conlon

ASTRONAUT SCHOOL

Wouldn't it be cool to go to Astronaut School,
to unravel the mysteries of space travel,
to find out what the universe is all about,
from the mathematics of rocket ships
to the science of a lunar eclipse?
Wouldn't it be brill to fill your head
with formulas for the right type of rocket fuel,
or for working out how much thrust
you must have to land safely on Mars?
Wouldn't it be great to practise
moonwalking in Games, and instead of French
learn Martian or Venusian.
knowing that someday, when your training was done,
you might even go where they're spoken?
Wouldn't it be fab to learn about lunar habitats,
to discover what grows in dust
or what stops rust on satellites?

All in all, it's clever stuff,
far too clever for me.
I'll just stay here and dream my way
through English, Maths and PE.

Brian Moses

ACKNOWLEDGEMENTS

'A Star Called Christa' © Debra Bertulis; 'The Winter Moon and the Willow' © Clare Bevan; 'Total Eclipse' © Valerie Bloom; 'Black Hole' © Liz Brownlee; 'Earthling! Do You Know What You Are?', 'Moon Landing: July 20th 1969', 'NOW…', 'Old As New', 'Space Poem', 'Thank You, Planet Theia…', 'The Moon Speaks!', 'The Shooting Stars', 'Universal Haiku Quartet' and 'What Are the Great Eight?' © James Carter; 'Black Hole' © Jane Clarke; 'From One Moon', 'Grains of Sand', 'The First Cosmonaut' and 'The Sun and the Hare' © Dom Conlon; 'Scalien' © Paul Cookson; 'Stars' © Pie Corbett; 'Space Doubt' and 'The First Man In Space' © Graham Denton; 'Fishes Are Stars' © Berlie Doherty; 'Moon Cat' and 'Recipe for Cosmic Cupcakes' © Julie Douglas; 'Perseids' © Sue Dymoke; 'Perseids' © Carrie Finison; 'Galileo (1564-1642)' © Chrissie Gittins; 'Dazzle Dance' and 'Stars' © Sue Hardy-Dawson. 'Dazzle Dance' was used previously for 'Light' (2015), a National Poetry Day film featuring fire performer Lydia Elisabeth Wild. It was also used on the Forward Poetry Arts Site linked to The Guardian; 'Flight From Planet Earth', 'The History of Nothing' and 'Tonight' © David Harmer; 'Moon' and 'The Point' © A.F. Harrold, reproduced by kind permission of the author; 'Headfirst Into Stars' © Karen G. Jordan; 'Imagine…' © Penny Kent, 2018; 'Galactic Waltz' © Tracey Mathias; 'Only the Moon' © Wong May; 'Silver Song' © B.J. Lee; 'Orange Star' © Linda

Lee Welch; 'Don't Just Google the Night Sky' © Joan McLellan; 'Welcome' © Trevor Millum; 'Discs and Dishes' © John Mole. First published in Catching the Spider by John Mole (Blackie, 1990); 'Astronaut School', 'Playing With Stars', 'Space Dog', 'The Aliens', 'The Great Galactic Ghoul' and 'The Intergalactic Holiday Bus' © Brian Moses; 'Moonscape' © Judith Nicholls. Published in Magic Mirror by Judith Nicholls (Faber & Faber, 1985), reprinted by permission of the author; 'First Dog on the Moon' © David Orme; 'The Aged Sun' and 'The Big Bang' © J. Patrick Lewis; 'Stargazing', 'The First Baby Born In Space' and 'The International Space Station Above Our House' © John Rice; 'Miranda the Frankenstein Moon' © Coral Rumble; 'Bang?' © Robert Schechter; 'Space Junk' © Joshua Seigal; 'Last Chance' © Kate Snow; 'The Monster That Ate the Universe' and 'Walking to the Stars' © Roger Stevens; 'Planet So-So' © Pauline Stewart; 'The Rise and Fall of Pluto' © Philip Waddell; 'Tiny Moon' © Zaro Weil; 'Comet Song' © Elli Woollard; 'George, Don't Do That' and 'Old Moon' © Bernard Young.

All efforts have been made to seek permission for copyright material, but in the event of any omissions, the publisher would be pleased to hear from the copyright holders and to amend these acknowledgements in subsequent editions.

INDEX OF FIRST LINES

birth of a star, The   88
boy once thought, A   52

Circling the earth   98
Coming out of school and there she is   20
Crumble a cluster of comets and a shower of meteorites   58

Daylight has toppled over the hills behind our house   99
Dear Moon, I shook my tendrils to tangle you   10

eerie light haloes the treetops, An   12

February 14, 3001   65
fictional space monster that was reputed, A   75
Fishes are stars   48
... for hurtling through the universe   39

Galaxies sing while Andromeda dances   60
giant plughole out in space, A   56

Hearing what I want to hear   89
Hi there, First Dog on the Moon   31
How old are you?   85

I am made of heat and light   64
I began with a pancake   68
I came to the Entry Desk   78

I heard about the first telescope 92
I, the moon 22
I'd been hanging around 43
If the sun was made of birthday cake 51
I'm looking out of my bedroom window 6
Imagine a planet 45
In an old black and white movie 33
Intergalactic Holiday Bus, The 41

Landing here because we had to 80
Lunar glare of cold silver 71

mammal with a massive brain, A 97
Moon Cat sits by the twisted tree 9
Moon is older than history 24
Moon, peer in my window 26
moon was but a Chin of Gold, The 21
My first could be hostile, it's always in space 74

No air, no mist, no man, no beast 32

Once there was nothing 90
One August night 62

Point to the sky 4

Scalien snakes through cosmic skies 77
She must have been someone's pet 95
Shuttle brought a midwife, The 102
Sometimes it feels like you can touch the moon 15

Stars are to reach for 49

Sudden shafts of light 61

sun is like a gold balloon, The 17

Sunshine melts away, frightened, when the cursing comets 72

That night we went out in the dark 3

There are more stars in the universe 8

There is an asteroid named Christa 101

There's MERCURY, VENUS 38

There's nothing as strange, showing unexplained change 47

They came to look round 83

They look across at the distant earth 28

They say that bits of rusty satellite 66

Tiny moon 27

To celebrate the first moonwalk 29

Travel through life 104

Upon a lake 50

Well, we thank you, Edwin Hubble 94

What does a comet sing of? 63

What's the matter 57

When I asked Dad 81

When I was a child I thought 23

When Sun was young 35

When the Big Bang banged 70

Whether our star, the sun, grows old 36

Wouldn't it be cool to go to Astronaut School 106

Wrap up warm and go outside, out into the darkness 5

Young children know what it's like 13

INDEX OF AUTHOR NAMES

Bertulis, Debra 101
Bevan, Clare 10
Bloom, Valerie 12
Brownlee, Liz 56

Carter, James 3, 17, 22, 29, 38,
  39, 71, 85, 88, 97
Clarke, Jane 57
Conlon, Dom 8, 28, 35, 104
Cookson, Paul 77
Corbett, Pie 49

Denton, Graham 81, 98
Dickinson, Emily 21
Doherty, Berlie 48
Douglas, Julie 9, 58
Dymoke, Sue 61

Finison, Carrie 62

Gittins, Chrissie 92

Hardy-Dawson, Sue 52, 64
Harmer, David 6, 80, 90
Harrold, A.F. 4, 20

Jordan, Karen G. 50

Kent, Penny 74

Lee, B.J. 26
Lee Welch, Linda 65
Lewis, J. Patrick 36, 94
Mathias, Tracey 60
May, Wong 23
McLellan, Joan 5
Millum, Trevor 78
Mole, John 89
Moses, Brian 13, 41, 75,
  83, 95, 106

Nicholls, Judith 32

Orme, David 31

Rice, John 51, 99, 102
Rumble, Coral 47

Schechter, Robert 70
Seigal, Joshua 66
Snow, Kate 72
Stevens, Roger 15, 68
Stewart, Pauline 45

Waddell, Philip 43
Weil, Zaro 27
Woollard, Elli 63

Young, Bernard 24, 33

For more from some of the brilliant poets
featured in this book visit:

www.bloomsbury.com

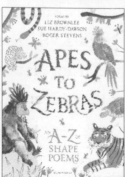
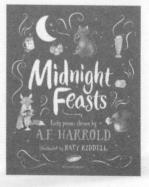

MORE FROM
JAMES CARTER

"A DREAMER?
ME? ERR, YOU BET,
THE WORLD'S
GREATEST
SPACE CADET!"

Join James Carter on a journey through space
and time: meet everyone from a Viking warrior
to a crazed cat — and travel from planer Earth
to the very edges of the universe...

Published by
Bloomsbury Education
ISBN 9781472929464